Looking *at* Pictures

Changing Colour

~ Joy Richardson ~

FRANKLIN WATTS

LONDON•SYDNEY

First published in Great Britain in 1997
This edition 1999
Franklin Watts
96 Leonard Street
London EC2A 4RH

Franklin Watts Australia
14 Mars Road
Lane Cove NSW 2066

0 7496 3569 X

10 9 8 7 6 5 4

Dewey Decimal Classification Number: 758

A CIP catalogue record for this book is
available from the British Library.

Editor: Sarah Ridley
Designer: Louise Thomas
Art Director: Robert Walster

Photographs:
©British Museum pgs 4-5; reproduced by courtesy of the Trustees of the National
Gallery, London Lotto/ Family Group pgs 6-7, Meléndez/Still Life pgs 8-9, Turner/The
Fighting Téméraire pgs 10-11, detail (pg 29), Monet/Water-Lily Pond pgs 14-15, 28
(detail), Seurat/Bathers at Asnières pgs 16-17, 26 (detail), van Gogh/Sunflowers cover,
pgs 18-19; ©RMN/Renoir/Dancing at the Moulin de la Galette pgs 12-
13/©RMN/Gauguin/The White Horse pgs 20-21, 29 (detail);©Succession André
Derain/DACS 1997, The Pool of London/©Tate Gallery, London pgs 22-23, ©Succession
Kandinsky/DACS 1997 Cossacks/ ©Tate Gallery, London pgs 24-25.

Printed in Belgium

Contents

How do you make brown?
What colour are shadows?
Which colours look good together?

Explore the pictures in this book to discover some artists' answers.

Hunting Birds
from Nebamun's tomb

Nebamun is out hunting.
These bright colours were painted
over three thousand years ago.

The painter probably had black, white, red, yellow and blue paint to use.

Which colours did he mix to make these browns?

Look at the colour patterns in the cat's fur ...

the bird's feathers and the fish's scales.

Family Group
painted by Lotto

Lotto showed off the best colours
in the front of this painting.

Colours were made from rocks, plants or insects. The best blues and reds cost a lot of money.

 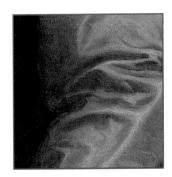 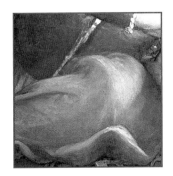

Look at the rosy red and rich blue clothes ...

and the brilliant colours in the carpet.

The sea and sky are a duller, cheaper blue.

Still Life
painted by Meléndez

In this collection of ordinary things,
the colours are arranged to look good together.

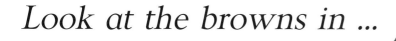

Look at the browns in ...

a barrel ...

a box ...

a jug ...

and some walnuts.

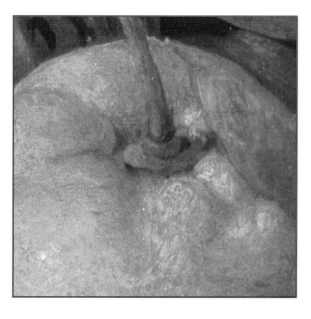

Are the oranges all the same colour?

How many different greens can you see?

The Fighting Téméraire
painted by Turner

Sunset colours set the scene
as the old ship is towed away.

Look at the sunset colours ...

reflected in the water ...

and on the
black steam tug.

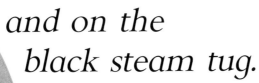

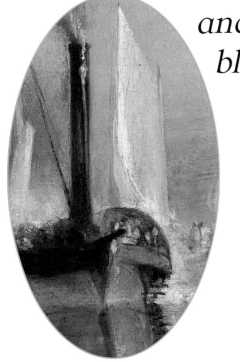

The old
sailing ship
is tinged
with gold.

Can you see the tiny, pale, new moon?

Dancing at the Moulin de la Galette
painted by Renoir

Renoir discovers dancing colours
at a sunlit party in the open air.

Look at the dappled colours
where sunshine filters
through the trees.

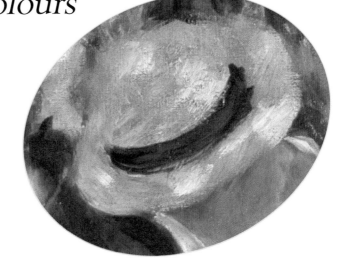

The dress
shimmers
and gleams.

The face
softly glows.

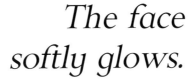

Blurry brush
strokes make colours
quiver in the light.

Renoir had
plenty of colours
to choose from.

The Water-Lily Pond
painted by Monet

Monet painted his pond again and again,
watching how colours changed with the light.

What colours are the willow trees?

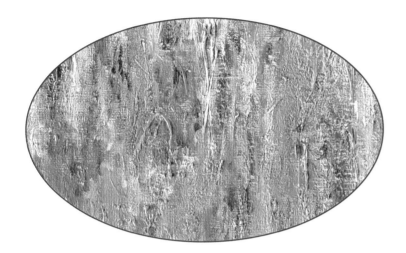

*Sunshine stripes
the green with gold.*

*What colour
is the bridge?*

What colour is the water?

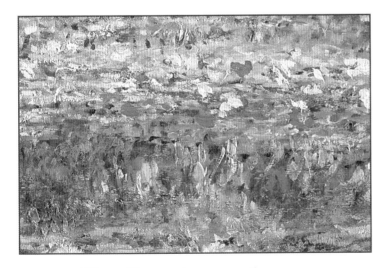

*Reflections hang
between the lily pads.*

*Purple shadows
hide the white.*

Bathers at Asnières
painted by Seurat

Thousands of strokes of colour
fill this picture like a mosaic.

Look at the colours in ...

shining water ...

grass
on the
bank ...

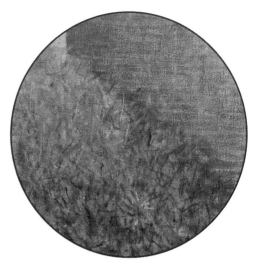

smoke in
the sky.

What colours can you
find in the shadows?

Sunflowers
painted by van Gogh

Van Gogh was excited by
the blazing yellow colours of sunflowers.

He painted the golden flowers
with a lemon background.
How many yellows can you see?

Look how brush
strokes of thick paint
make drooping petals ...

and bumpy seed heads.

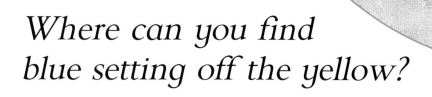

Where can you find
blue setting off the yellow?

The White Horse
painted by Gauguin

Gauguin paints a magical world
of animals, plants and people
in colourful harmony.

The white horse mirrors the colours of the forest.

The red horse stands out against the green.

The grey horse merges into the shadows.

Flowers bloom in the dark undergrowth.

The Pool of London
painted by André Derain

Derain uses strong, bright colours
in this scene to make a lively picture.

Look at his colour patchwork.

He put colours
together carefully.

Look for red and
green,

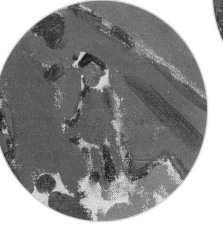

blue and
orange,

yellow and
mauve.

The colours in these
pairs are opposite
colours. They brighten
each other up.

He sets everything off
with green sea and sky.

Cossacks
painted by Kandinsky

Soldiers are fighting a battle.
Colours and lines give the feeling.

Fur-hatted soldiers march with lances.

Swords slash and horses clash.

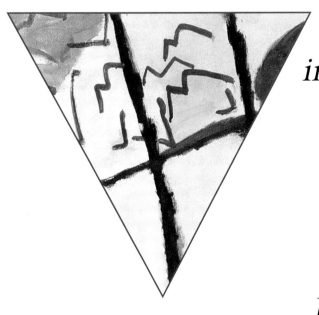

Birds fly off
in a flurry.

Look at the
rainbow bridging the valley.

Painting with Colour

Colour circle

Red, yellow and blue are called the primary colours.
Other colours fit between them, like the colours of the rainbow.

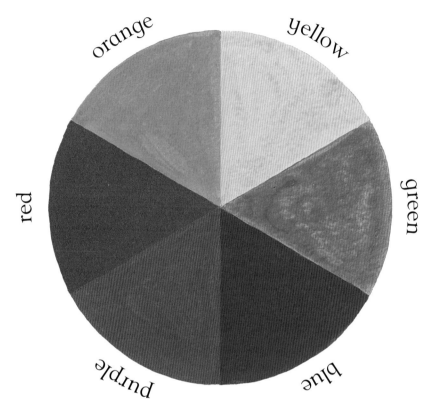

orange · yellow · green · blue · purple · red

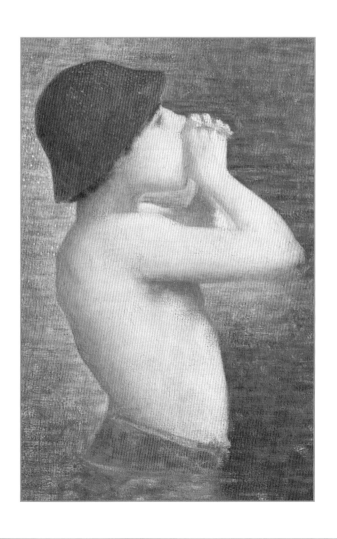

Try making this colour circle. Start with the primary colours. Then mix each pair of primary colours together to make the colour between them.

Opposites, like blue and orange, can make each other look brighter.

For help, look back at pages 16 and 22.

Colour count

How many colours can you make by mixing two colours together?

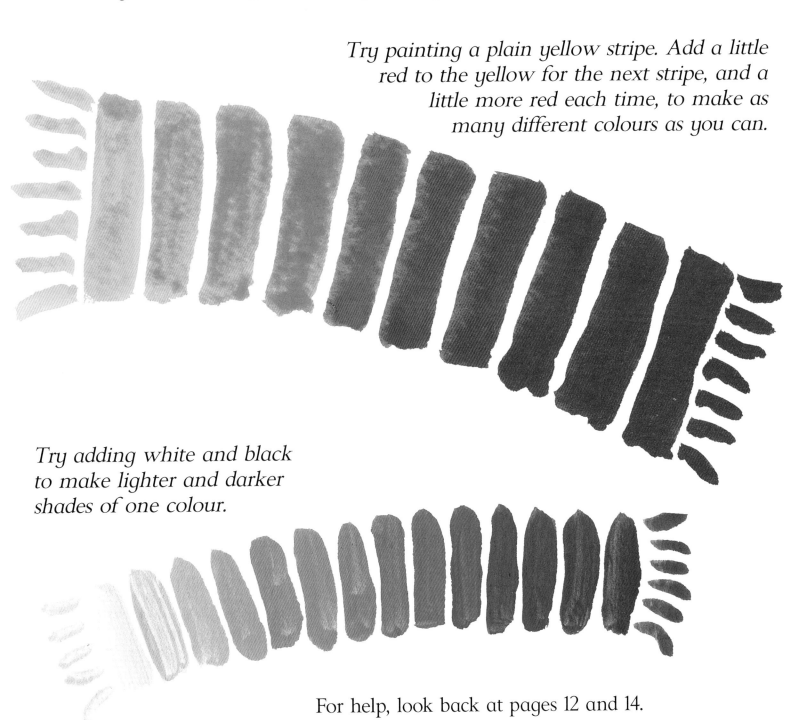

Try painting a plain yellow stripe. Add a little red to the yellow for the next stripe, and a little more red each time, to make as many different colours as you can.

Try adding white and black to make lighter and darker shades of one colour.

For help, look back at pages 12 and 14.

Making brown

Make a collection of brown things.
Using red, yellow, blue,
black and white paint,
can you mix colours
to match each
brown?

For help, look back at pages 4 and 8.

Merging colours

Strokes of colour painted close together merge when seen from a distance.

Try painting grass, or leaves
on a tree, with brush strokes
of different colours.

For help, look back at pages 14 and 16.

Colour feelings

Colours affect our feelings.
They give a picture its mood.

*Draw a simple picture twice over.
Paint one picture with colours to
make it look cheerful and the
other with gloomy colours.*

For help, look back at pages 10, 18 and 20.

Colour change

*Make your own colour
arrangement.
Paint a shell, a face, a
tree or a cloudy sky with
surprise colours which
look good together.*

For help, look back at pages 22 and 24.

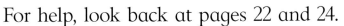

More about the pictures in this book

Hunting Birds

Nebamun was an official in ancient Egypt. This scene was painted on a wall of his tomb around 1400 BC. It shows him on the marshes in a papyrus boat, with his wife and daughter. The painter used colours made from powdered minerals.

Family Group

Lorenzo Lotto (about 1480-1556) worked in Venice. He wrote in his account book that this portrait was valued at fifty ducats 'judged for quality and the finest colours'. The best colours were expensive and hard to come by. The finest blue, made from the mineral lapis lazuli, cost more than gold.

Still Life with Oranges and Walnuts

Luis Meléndez (1716-1780) came from a family of Spanish painters. He tried, but failed, to gain a post at the royal court, and he died in poverty. He was a brilliant still-life painter, down to the smallest detail. You can even see the woodworm holes in this table.

The Fighting Téméraire

Joseph Mallord William Turner (1775-1851) was impressed by the sight of this old sailing ship, which had fought in the Battle of Trafalgar (1805), being towed away by a modern steam tug. The colours set the mood as the sunset salutes a splendid past, and the new moon rises over a world which is moving on.

Dancing at the Moulin de la Galette

Pierre Auguste Renoir (1841-1919) was a French impressionist painter. This picture is like a kaleidoscope of shifting colours. Unlike painters in earlier centuries, Renoir and his friends could choose from a huge range of cheap machine-made colours, and carry their paints around with them in metal tubes.

The Water-Lily Pond

Claude Monet (1840-1926) set out to paint the impression of what he really saw, rather than what he knew or remembered. He built this Japanese-style bridge over the pond in his garden, and he painted the same view many times, delighting in the ever-changing colours.

■ Bathers at Asnières

Georges Seurat (1859-1891) painted this huge picture. It is 2 metres by 3 metres, and the foreground figures are almost life-size. Seurat planned every detail from sketches. He achieved his colour effects by patiently laying countless strokes of blended colour beside each other. Later, he went further and began to make his paintings from dots of pure colour.

■ Sunflowers

Vincent van Gogh (1853-1890) wanted to paint pictures of sunflowers to decorate the house at Arles in France, which he moved into in 1888. Over the summer, he painted five with yellow backgrounds. Colours carried strong feelings for van Gogh. He frequently used yellow in his paintings, often balanced by blue.

■ The White Horse

Paul Gauguin (1848-1903) left France in 1891 and went to live on the South Pacific island of Tahiti, where he painted this picture. He believed that artists should study nature but paint from their imagination. He chose colours to catch the mood and to make the picture look good, rather than to show what he saw.

■ The Pool of London

André Derain (1880-1954) was French but he painted this picture in England. He put Tower Bridge in the background as a helpful landmark. Derain was interested in new theories about colour contrasts, and used these to make the picture more vivid. People were shocked at first and called painters like Derain *Les Fauves* (the wild beasts).

■ Cossacks

Wassily Kandinsky (1866-1944) was Russian. This painting was made in 1911 and it shows Cossacks (Russian cavalry) fighting. Kandinsky was a pioneer of abstract painting, exploring the way that colours and forms can express emotions without representing recognisable things. Here, you can pick out soldiers and weapons, but the sense of chaos and conflict is made by the colours, shapes and titlting lines.

Index